# The Ultimate Motorcycles

# CUSTOM BIKES

Lori Kinstad Pupeza

ABDO Publishing Company

## visit us at
## www.abdopub.com

Published by Abdo Publishing Company 4940 Viking Drive, Edina, Minnesota 55435.
Copyright © 1998 by Abdo Consulting Group, Inc. International copyrights reserved in all
countries. No part of this book may be reproduced in any form without written permission
from the publisher.

Printed in the United States.

Photo credits: AP/Wide World, SuperStock, Peter Arnold, Inc., Yamaha

Edited by Kal Gronvall

### Library of Congress Cataloging-in-Publication Data

Pupeza, Lori Kinstad
   Custom bikes / Lori Kinstad Pupeza.
      p.  cm. -- (The ultimate motorcycle series)
  Includes index.
  Summary: Discusses the history, riding, and racing of custom bikes, including such
aspects as the engine, other parts, gear, and safety tips.
   ISBN 1-57765-000-X
   1. Motorcycles--Customizing--Juvenile literature. [1.Motorcycles--Customizing.] I.
Title. II. Series: Pupeza, Lori Kinstad. Ultimate motorcycle series
  TL440.15.P87 1998
  629.227'5--dc21

                                         97-53097
                                            CIP
                                              AC

**Warning:** The series *The Ultimate Motorcycles* is intended as entertainment for
children. These activities should never be attempted without training, instruction,
supervision, and proper equipment.

# Contents

# The Art of Customizing

*The* art of customizing is all about personalizing a motorcycle to fit the owner's needs and style. One person might put a fairing on their bike to block the wind on long rides. Another will spend a lot of time and money to have flames painted on his or her motorcycle's gas tank. Still another will chrome all the engine parts.

Some people like to add things to their motorcycles that make long rides more comfortable. Improving engine performance is another reason for modification. Others put up with considerable discomfort for the sake of appearance. Changing the bike to fit the owner—whatever the need—is just part of the fun of owning a motorcycle.

There are probably as many reasons for customizing a motorcycle as there are motorcycle owners. People change their motorcycles for lots of reasons. There is never a wrong way to do it. Motorcyclists modify their bikes to fit their own personalities. There isn't a set of plans on how to customize a motorcycle. It is all up to the individual to decide what he or she needs to make the motorcycle more comfortable, perform better, or look nicer.

Customizing a bike—making it better than it was—has been done since motorcycles were first invented. Although early modifications by inventors focused more on the performance of the machine, styles were refashioned again and again throughout the years. Every curve of the exhaust pipe and each adjustment to the handlebars made for a better handling, more stylish motorcycle.  Decade after decade, new designs hit the showroom floor, wowing potential customers.  Altering every inch of the chassis and everything attached to it became an exciting race between manufacturers.

Older motorcycles sometimes are customized for easier driving.  Older motorcycles that are only equipped with a kick start can have an electric start added for more convenience.  Disc brakes can replace the slower, less smooth drum brakes for quicker stopping.  Some motorcycle enthusiasts don't want to change anything on a bike, and go to great lengths to restore a motorcycle to its original condition.  Not customizers, they want the bike to fit their needs and their tastes.

**Some people look just as funny as their bikes.**

# The Flash Factor

*One* reason people modify their motorcycles is to make them look different from any other motorcycles on the road. Intense colors and polished chrome make these bikes look more like pieces of shiny machine art rather than simple transportation. Beautiful air brush paintings and pin striping change the look of the bike dramatically. Smaller changes, like adding chrome nuts and bolts, can add just the right touch. Some machines are so customized that they don't ever touch the pavement. They're towed on trailers to rallies and bike shows, only to be rolled off a ramp and on to showroom carpet.

Paint can give a factory bike a whole new look. Bold patterns and hand painted detail make a big impression. Owners sometimes spend over a thousand dollars on paint alone. The most detailed jobs can take months. Some owners like flames of different colors to wrap around the gas tank. Others prefer the side of the tank to have a picture or a name painted across it. A professional paint job will make a motorcycle stand out, but that's not the only thing a customized bike needs.

Chrome adds the finishing touch. It is probably the most noticeable thing on a motorcycle. There are two ways to get more chrome on a motorcycle: have someone chrome plate the parts

that are already on the bike, or buy parts that are already chromed. Cyclists can purchase chrome accessory parts from specialty shops. Chrome plating is also a good way to customize a motorcycle. It is usually less expensive than buying a whole different chromed part.

The process of chroming takes a lot of work. There are three different steps to the process. The piece being chromed is first dipped into copper, then nickel, and finally chrome. If done correctly, a chromed surface will reflect like a mirror. Almost every part of the engine can be chrome plated. Some motorcycles even have chrome gas tanks.

*Paint and chrome are the most common ways of adding flash to a motorcycle.*

# Power!

Modifying the engine can make a motorcycle cruise down the road with more power.  All four-stroke motorcycle engines work basically the same way. They are turned on by either an electric start push button, or a kick start. Most bikes built since the late 1960s and into the 1970s have electric starts.

To start the engine, gas and air go into the cylinder.  The gas is compressed by a piston and ignited when the ignition makes a spark.  This explosion makes the gas expand, pushing the piston downwards. The exhaust exits the cylinder into an exhaust pipe. The crankshaft changes the up and down movement into a circular one.  The four strokes of a piston are intake, compression, power, and exhaust.

The power created by the internal combustion engine is transferred to the rear wheel by either a chain, a belt, or a shaft. Whatever method is used, it makes it possible for the power from the engine to push the bike along the road.  Custom bike owners will sometimes put a fancy cover over the chain, which is called the primary case cover.

Customizers can change the size of the engine parts, like the flywheel and the piston rods, to make a bigger stroke.  This makes the engine more powerful and faster. Changing the size of the

flywheel is similar to changing the sprocket size on a bicycle. A bigger sprocket will give more speed once a bike is moving than a smaller sprocket could. The engine becomes more efficient at higher speeds with a bigger flywheel.

Making the bike run smoother can be done with few changes. Changing the chain to a belt is one way to do this. An extra-wide belt gives optimum power transfer from the engine to the back wheel.

Making changes to the engine takes a lot of knowledge. Kits are available that have all the parts needed to customize the engine. Adding different parts isn't the only thing done when customizing an engine. Many parts need to be re-calibrated and adjusted. Valves have to be changed to be in sync with the rest of the engine. Even though it's a lot of hard work, customizers consider it a labor of love.

*There is no limit to how much an engine can be customized.*

# *Choppers*

*Customizing* a motorcycle is a very individual choice, but one style of customized motorcycles caught on in the 1960s and is still popular today. The "Chopper" look is definitely here to stay. The long, extended front forks and the "ape-hanger" handlebars have become the defining look of the rebel biker.

Harley-Davidson motorcycles have the reputation for becoming choppers, but this type of customizing has been done to just about every kind of motorcycle. From the Japanese-made Honda to the British-born Triumph, every two-wheeled machine has been "chop-ified."

These modifications, however, are only made for show. Choppers aren't the easiest things to drive. The extra-long forks throw off the balance of the bike, and taking turns can be tricky.

*Actress Ann Margret donated her Harley-Davidson Spider Motorcycle to the new Las Vegas Harley Davidson Cafe in 1997. Harley-Davidson motorcycles are best known for the "chopper" look, but any motorcycle can become a chopper.*

# The Practical Side

*Some* people change their bikes for practical reasons. Changing the seat or adding a back rest can make a long road trip more comfortable. A large fairing can be added to block wind and cold. Some drivers have luggage racks and gas tank bags specially made to fit their bike. For safety reasons, owners add bigger, brighter head and tail lights. Although these changes aren't always very attractive, they serve the driver's purposes.

The old saying, "necessity is the mother of invention" is definitely true of sidecars. Something all motorcycles have in common is their lack of passenger space. Although some motorcycles come with an optional stock sidecar, most do not.

Owners modify salvaged sidecars to match the motorcycle as closely as possible. Customizers paint it the same color as the bike and give it similar accessories. People go to great lengths to have pieces hand made to match the motorcycle. Owners will spend years looking for just the right fender or tail light to fit their machine or sidecar.

Those who aren't physically able to drive a stock motorcycle can have levers and pedals moved around according to their needs. Just as in cars, customizers can adjust every control on the bike. The position of the brake and clutch lever, and the brake and shift pedals aren't the same on every bike. American,

Japanese, and Italian bikes usually have the throttle and the front brake lever on the right handlebar. The clutch lever sits on the left handlebar. The right foot pedal controls the back brake, and the left foot pedal is the shifter. On some British bikes, the controls on the left and right sides are reversed.

Like every other part of the motorcycle, these too can be changed. Making the bike into what the motorcyclist wants it to be is what matters to a customizer. The idea of modifying what already exists has probably been around since the time the first motorcycle was invented.

**This bike was customized for the comfort of the rider to make long trips easier.**

# The Parts of a Custom Bike

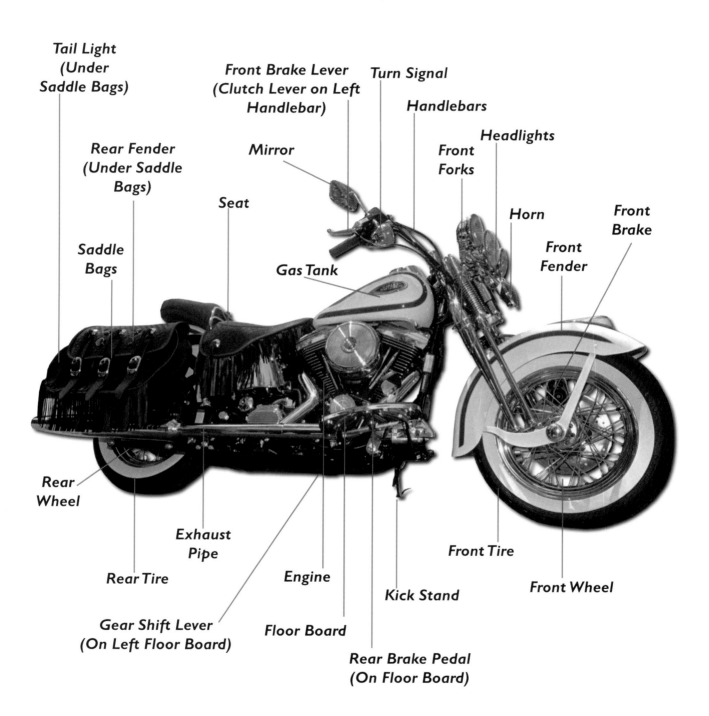

Tail Light
(Under
Saddle Bags)

Front Brake Lever
(Clutch Lever on Left
Handlebar)

Turn Signal

Handlebars

Rear Fender
(Under Saddle
Bags)

Mirror

Headlights

Front
Forks

Seat

Horn

Front
Brake

Saddle
Bags

Gas Tank

Front
Fender

Rear
Wheel

Exhaust
Pipe

Engine

Front Tire

Rear Tire

Kick Stand

Front Wheel

Gear Shift Lever
(On Left Floor Board)

Floor Board

Rear Brake Pedal
(On Floor Board)

# How a Four-Stroke Engine Works

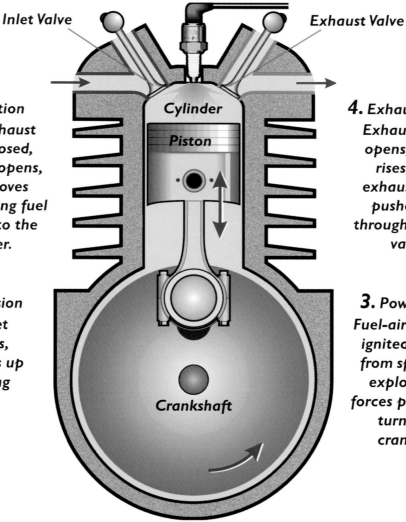

Spark Plug

Inlet Valve

Exhaust Valve

**1.** Induction stroke: Exhaust valve is closed, inlet valve opens, piston moves down drawing fuel and air into the cylinder.

Cylinder

Piston

**4.** Exhaust stroke: Exhaust valve opens, piston rises, used exhaust gas is pushed out through exhaust valve.

**2.** Compression stroke: Inlet valve closes, piston moves up compressing fuel-air mixture.

Crankshaft

**3.** Power stroke: Fuel-air mixture is ignited by spark from spark plug, exploding gas forces piston down turning the crankshaft.

# The First Motorcycles

*Today's* motorcycles don't look anything like the first inventions of a motorized bicycle. The very first motorcycles were surprisingly simple. Simple engines were fit onto bicycle frames. In 1869, three men put together the first motorized bicycle. In their workshop, Ernest Michaux, Pierre Michaux, and Louis Guillaume Perreaux took a chance at attaching a steam engine to the frame of a bicycle. They attached a belt from the engine to the back wheel to propel the wheel. On the first test drive, the steam-driven bicycle made it about 10 miles (16 km). The driver must have had a hot ride because he had to sit right on top of the engine's boiler! The invention was a hit all over the world.

Cyclists tried different ways of propelling their bikes. One invention used clockwork power. This didn't work very well because the engine had to be wound every hundred yards or so. This made it hard for the driver to get anywhere quickly. Another inventor thought it would be a good idea to use dogs to push the bicycle forward. He called it the Cynosphere. It was a tricycle that had cages for its back two wheels. Small dogs ran in the cages, pushing the wheels forward, like the way a hamster runs in a wheel. The inventor didn't pursue this motorcycle because it didn't work. The dogs didn't always want to run when their driver

wanted them to. The dogs would tire and needed food and water. Although these ideas didn't work out very well, they all played a part in making a better machine. As any customizer knows, sometimes it takes many tries to make something work.

Inventors tried to improve the steam-driven motorcycle by rearranging the placement of the engine or changing things on the bicycle. They soon found that nothing pushed a bicycle along quite as well as the internal combustion engine. In 1876, a German engineer named Nikolaus Otto built the first internal combustion engine. This led to the first gasoline-driven motorcycle.

*This 1949 NSU Fox is an early relative to the modern motorcycle.*

In 1885, two Germans, Gottleib Daimler and Wilhelm Maybach, put a similar engine onto a wooden frame. Like the first steam-driven motorcycle, the Daimler motorcycle made it 10 exciting miles (16 km) down the road. During this ride, the seat caught on fire because it was too close to the hot engine! New plans had to be made to solve new problems. These two men adjusted things until the bike worked better.

# More Modifications

*Despite* the design problems, people all over the world were excited about driving the two-wheeled wonders. Inventors of the Daimler motorcycle decided it was time to manufacture a motorcycle to sell to the public. Only nine years after their first try at building a motorcycle, Daimler and Maybach became partners with Alois Wolfmuller to mass produce motorcycles. They built a twin-cylinder, four-stroke motorcycle. It went up to speeds of only 24 miles per hour (38 kmph). At first, people loved the motorcycles, and in only two short years they had sold 1,000 of them.

Unfortunately, the motorcycles weren't built very well. People stopped buying them because the motorcycles weren't dependable means of transportation. In 1897, the factory shut down, and the inventors made no more motorcycles.

Early bike designers—the first customizers—couldn't find the right place to put the engine. Some put the engine at the rear, with a bar attached to the seat. Others put the engine on a trolley, which the motorcycle pulled behind on a third wheel. Another design had the engine above the front wheel. This made it hard to steer. In 1901, designers of the Werner Bike put the engine between the wheels. Today's motorcycles are based on this design.

There were many different small companies constantly redesigning motorcycles. Motorcycles were a new invention, and everyone wanted to try and manufacture the best design before anybody else did. Because of this competition, in only 15 years, motorcycles had gone from awkward, extravagant toys, to practical, well-designed machines.

*This mechanic is checking to make sure everything on this motorcycle is running and sounding right.*

# Harley-Davidson

*During* the first few decades of the invention of the motorcycle, companies popped up over night to develop the best motorcycle. Around 1900, motorcyclists needed reliable, sturdy machines that would make it across America's open, undeveloped, rugged terrain. Motorcycle manufacturers customized bikes to handle the conditions these settlers faced. People were just beginning to see how fun and practical these two-wheeled wonders really were.

About this time, two American school friends, William Harley and Arthur Davidson, started to build their first motorcycle in a wooden shed in the backyard of the Davidson's home. Harley was a draftsman at an engineering company and Davidson was a pattern maker. In 1903, they finished their first motorcycle. What they didn't know is that their motorcycle would someday be one of the most popular bikes in the world. The motorcycle they were building had a 400 cc single-cylinder engine that fit into a bicycle frame. It proved to be mechanically well-built, but too slow. Harley redesigned the engine and gave it 475 cc's.

In 1904, Harley-Davidson manufactured the "Silent Gray Fellow." The "Silent Gray Fellow" is a far cry from today's chrome covered Harley-Davidsons. They called it "Silent" because its

mufflers were designed to run quietly, "Gray" because it was painted gray, and "Fellow" because Harley-Davidson wanted drivers to think of these bikes as their reliable friends. They wanted their motorcycles to be trusted, durable machines.

*Harley-Davidson motorcycles have come a long way since the "Silent Gray Fellow," but they are still considered one of the finest motorcycles available. Here Senator Ken Chlouber of Colorado gets off of his 1995 Harley on his way to work in the Colorado Legislature.*

# World War II

**During** the 1930s, not as many motorcycles were being produced because of the Depression. Most people couldn't afford to buy motorcycles, and most companies couldn't stay in business to build them. Then World War II began, and soon United States involvement couldn't be postponed any longer. The government started to prepare for war. America's soldiers needed dependable, fuel-efficient transportation. So Harley-Davidson and Indian were asked to build military motorcycles.

Indian responded with the Indian 841. It was a V-twin, mounted so the cylinders stuck out on the sides. It also was shaft-driven, rather than chain- or belt-driven, which made for easier riding in desert conditions. Not many were used in the war because they weren't developed fast enough. Most of these motorcycles were sold to civilians and were eventually used as street bikes.

*The V-twin engine is simply 2 four-stroke cylinders set at an angle from each other and working together for more power.*

The Harley-Davidson WLA proved to be more helpful on the battlefield. The bike was painted olive drab green with "U.S. Army" stenciled on the tank. Some bikes had sidecars, so one soldier could ride in the sidecar and shoot a mounted gun while another soldier drove. It came equipped with a large luggage rack on the back to carry the 40 pound (18 kg) radios used in the field. A gun holder, called a scabbard, was mounted next to the front fork. The bikes had to be modified to accommodate the soldiers' needs.

At the end of World War II, the soldiers returned to America wanting to start a new life. They had either seen or ridden on the military bikes, and many wanted one of their own. Sales improved in the 1950s. The 1950s brought on a whole new wave of motorcycles. People wanted to have fun, and motorcycle sales were booming. By 1955, Japanese bikes like Honda, Kawasaki, Yamaha, and Suzuki earned respect and popularity because they were very reliable machines.

*By the late 1950s the Japanese began making motorcycles that had the stylish look of an American custom bike crossed with the reliability of a Japanese bike.*

Fun was becoming the key word in motorcycling. They weren't just needed for military purposes or for practical transportation. The motorcycle was still used for cheap transportation, but owners wanted their bikes to represent who they were. They wanted their bikes to reflect their personalities. A new era brought new trends. Times were turning wild, and this was reflected in the way people turned their bikes into art, or at the very least, something a little different than what factories churned out. Art imitated life, and motorcyclists took their machines to the edge.

During the 1960s and into the 1970s, choppers became popular motorcycles. Harley-Davidson had made a name for itself, and the company was going strong. In the 1980s, the company decided to make motorcycles that resembled these customized bikes and sell them. People who wanted the look of a custom bike, but didn't have the time or know-how to build a custom bike, could walk into a Harley-Davidson dealership and buy one to their tastes. These bikes are called factory customs.

*Opposite page: (Top) Harley-Davidsons are considered factory customs because each bike is made to how the customer orders it. (Bottom) The new 1997 Harley-Davidson Heritage Springer Softail was designed to look just like the 1948 Panhead.*

# *Hybrid Bikes*

*The* name "custom bikes" might conjure pictures of the American-built chopper, but custom bikes are big all over the world. Because of the high cost of Harley-Davidson motorcycles, people are customizing every kind of motorcycle. Some like the challenge of restoring an old Honda or Suzuki. They're easy bikes to come by, and are a good, inexpensive bike on which to learn.

In Europe, it's very common to see a Triumph or a Norton customized to the extreme like a Harley-Davidson. Mixing and matching parts from different motorcycle companies can be done with a little imagination. Doing this can make for a better bike overall.

For example, Norton motorcycles are known for making a sturdy frame, but their engines are not as efficient or reliable as their Japanese counterparts. Some customizers find the "cross breed" motorcycle is a better bike all around. They use only the best parts, and throw away the bad parts. This kind of motorcycle is harder to build because parts from different manufacturers are completely different and are hard to fit together. Owners go as far as to fabricate their own pieces. This takes a lot of skill, but is sometimes the only option in extreme custom jobs. Attaching a

Kawasaki engine to a Triumph transmission is a tough job. But with patience and mechanical ability, owners have successfully created hybrid bikes.

*Some motorcycles are so customized that they sometimes don't look much like a motorcycle. Adam Petty (grandson of race car driver Richard Petty) rode this monster cycle at the Charlotte Motor Speedway in North Carolina on Oct. 2, 1995.*

# A Lifetime of Fun

*To* see the most extreme custom jobs, go to a motorcycle show. They are held all over the world and display some of the wildest, craziest, and most beautiful pieces of work ever. Contests are held every year to decide who went the farthest with their custom jobs.

Learning about custom bikes can be a lot of fun. Check out a custom bike or specialty shop to get an up-close look at how people build custom bikes. There are lots of reasons people customize their motorcycles. Some owners want to steal the spotlight at a motorcycle rally, others just want a comfortable ride down the road.

Ask any customizer what his or her reasons are for modifying an already perfectly good bike, and there won't be two answers alike. Customizing can be anything the owner wants. There's no right or wrong way to do it.

Some custom jobs entail a minor change of mirrors or hand grips. Others take years and thousands of dollars and end up looking nothing like the original motorcycle. The fun of customizing a motorcycle lies in the endless possibilities of how a bike will turn out. Customizers spend a lifetime turning hunks of steel into rolling pieces of art.

**Cook Harald Ricken poses with the famed "Florida Hamburger Trike" in Essen, Germany in 1995. The owner Harry Sperl spent 19 months and $100,000 to build this one of a kind cycle.**

# *Glossary*

**CC (Cubic Centimeters)** - used to measure the size of an engine.

**Chain Driven** - a chain is used to transfer the power from the engine to the rear wheel.

**Chassis** - the frame of the bike made out of steel or carbon fiber.

**Clutch** - connects the power from the engine to the transmission.

**Crankshaft** - the part of the engine that changes the up and down movement of the piston into a circular movement.

**Cylinder** - the piston chamber of the engine.

**Disc Brake** - brakes that are a single disc that are squeezed to a stop.

**Drum Brake** - An older technology where the brake is shaped like a drum.

**Fairing** - the covers on the sides and front of a motorcycle.

**Front Forks** - the front suspension that is shaped like a fork.

**Kick Start** - a way of starting the bike by kicking a lever down.

**Manufacturer** - a company that makes something in large numbers.

**Optimum** - the greatest or best way to attain something.

**Piston** - the part that moves up and down in the shaft of the cylinder.

**Sprocket** - the round disc with teeth that the chain wraps around.

**Swing Arm** - the part of the frame that the wheel sits in, and also acts as part of the suspension.

**Transmission** - the system that transfers the power from the engine to the rear wheel.

**Twin-Cylinder Engine** - two cylinders.

**V-Twin Engine** - two cylinders that sit vertically in a V formation.

# Internet Sites

### Minibike Central
http://www.geocities.com/MotorCity/7029/mini.html
This page shows pictures of awesome bikes and tells how to make them. It also has plenty of photos of minibikes and minicycles. This site will give you information on where to find minibikes and parts.

### Pete's SOLO Disabled Motorcycle Project
http://www.btinternet.com/~chaloner/pete/pete.htm
This website is about a different kind of custom bike. The page is for disabled people who want to ride a motorcycle. See photos of this customized bike, and how it works.

### The Dirt Bike Pages
http://www.off-road.com/orcmoto.html
This site has action photos of all kinds of dirt bikes, monthly columns and articles, and product reports. This site has important riding information, too.

### Scooter Magazine Online
http://www2.scootermag.it/scooter/
This web site is fully devoted to motorscooters. Technique, developments, new models, tests, track and road trials.

### The Motorcycle Database
http://www.motorcycle.informaat.nl/ehome.html
Over 250 motorcycles, their specifications and pictures, and driver experiences from visitors. Pick the model and year of motorcycle you would like to see. Photos and detailed information is included. Lots to see!

# Pass It On

Motorcycle Enthusiasts: educate readers around the country by passing on information you've learned about motorcycles. Share your little-known facts and interesting stories. Tell others what your favorite kind of motorcycle is or what your favorite type of riding is. We want to hear from you!

To get posted on the ABDO Publishing Company website E-mail us at
**"Sports@abdopub.com"**

**Visit the ABDO Publishing Company website at www.abdopub.com**

# Index